HAL•LEONARD
INSTRUMENTAL
PLAY-ALONG

CLARINET

AUDIO
ACCESS
INCLUDED

PLAYBACK+
Speed • Pitch • Balance • Loop

Disney
BEAUTY AND THE BEAST

ISBN 978-1-4950-9610-5

Wonderland Music Company, Inc.
Walt Disney Music Company

DISTRIBUTED BY

HAL•LEONARD®
7777 W. BLUEMOUND RD. P.O. BOX 13819 MILWAUKEE, WI 53213

In Australia Contact:
Hal Leonard Australia Pty. Ltd.
4 Lentara Court
Cheltenham, Victoria, 3192 Australia
Email: ausadmin@halleonard.com.au

Visit Hal Leonard Online at
www.halleonard.com

ARIA

CLARINET

Music by ALAN MENKEN
Lyrics by TIM RICE

BE OUR GUEST

CLARINET

Music by ALAN MENKEN
Lyrics by HOWARD ASHMAN

BEAUTY AND THE BEAST

CLARINET

Music by ALAN MENKEN
Lyrics by HOWARD ASHMAN

BELLE

CLARINET

Music by ALAN MENKEN
Lyrics by HOWARD ASHMAN

DAYS IN THE SUN

CLARINET

Music by ALAN MENKEN
Lyrics by TIM RICE

EVERMORE

CLARINET

Music by ALAN MENKEN
Lyrics by TIM RICE

GASTON

CLARINET

Music by ALAN MENKEN
Lyrics by HOWARD ASHMAN

HOW DOES A MOMENT LAST FOREVER

Clarinet

Music by ALAN MENKEN
Lyrics by TIM RICE

THE MOB SONG

CLARINET

Music by ALAN MENKEN
Lyrics by HOWARD ASHMAN

SOMETHING THERE

CLARINET

Music by ALAN MENKEN
Lyrics by HOWARD ASHMAN